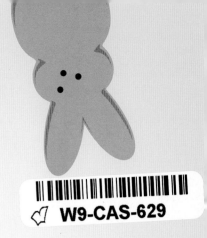

Peeps!

BRAND

Recipes and Crafts to Make
with Your Favorite Marshmallow Treat

By Charity Ferreira
Photographs by Liz Wolfe

CHRONICLE BOOKS
SAN FRANCISCO

Library of Congress Cataloging-in-Publication Data:
Ferreira, Charity.
Peeps! : recipes and crafts to make with your favorite marshmallow treat /
By Charity Ferreira ; photographs by Liz Wolfe.
p. cm.
Includes index.
ISBN-13: 978-0-8118-6041-3
ISBN-10: 0-8118-6041-8
1. Cookery (Marshmallow) I. Title.

TX799.F47 2008
641.8'53—dc22

2007016009

Manufactured in China
Designed by Tracy Sunrize Johnson

10 9 8 7 6 5 4 3 2 1

Chronicle Books LLC
680 Second Street
San Francisco, California 94107

www.chroniclebooks.com

CONTENTS

INTRODUCTION

Like most kids in the 1970s, I had a sweet tooth that could not be sated. The sweeter—and the more brightly colored—the better, was my motto. Luckily there was no shortage of weird and wacky sugar bombs at the neighborhood variety store where my friends and I spent all of our allowances. But even as jaded and candy-obsessed as I was, I always felt there was something different about PEEPS brand marshmallow candies.

No doubt my ardor was fueled by the fact that they were only available at certain times of the year. It probably also had something to do with their squat, improbably cute shape and their doe-eyed, mouthless expressions that managed to look both innocent and wise. Their slightly mysterious origins plus the wonder of how they were extruded into such neat little rows no doubt piqued my imagination and had something to do with my future as a pastry chef. Whatever the reasons, my brother and I devoured them fresh, stale, frozen, and microwaved. Finding them in our Easter baskets was a true rite of spring.

My childhood cronies and I are grown-ups now, but we still have a soft spot for PEEPS, and we're in good company. The Internet is a virtual gallery of cult-like dedication to the classic sugar-dusted Chicks and

Bunnies—over 200 unofficial Web sites in all! A little browsing turns up poems and songs, dioramas, paintings, sculptures, photo essays, and science experiments. One artist used thousands of PEEPS to create installation art pieces, one of which was an exhibit at COPIA: The American Center for Wine, Food & the Arts in Napa, California. Another awe-inspiring tribute is a scene-by-scene re-creation of the *Lord of the Rings* movie, with costumed PEEPS playing the roles of Frodo and friends. Computer game fans can even play Flash-animated games in which PEEPS are the stars. And the owner of one of my favorite fan sites has a blue neon PEEPS sculpture, commissioned especially for her by her girlfriend.

Though I like to think it was those of us who grew up in the '70s that became the most fiendish fans and made PEEPS the edible cultural

icons that they are today, PEEPS predate my generation. In the 1950s, Just Born, a Bethlehem, Pennsylvania, confectionery manufacturer (founded by Russian immigrant Sam Born, who learned the art of chocolate making in France and started with a small shop in New York City in 1923), bought the Rodda Candy Company of Lancaster, Pennsylvania. Among Rodda's products was a little yellow marshmallow Chick that their candy makers piped by hand with a pastry bag. Intrigued by these little curly-winged cuties, Just Born developed technology to mechanize their production, and the PEEPS brand went on to become the biggest nonchocolate Easter candy in the United States. Today, the PEEPS brand has expanded to include Easter Bunnies and eggs as well as a variety of shapes, colors, and flavors for Halloween, Christmas, and Valentine's Day. Believe it or not, there are even sugar-free PEEPS!

Whether you count yourself among the casual fans or the dedicated fanatics, this book is full of fun, silly, and tasty things you can do with your favorite candy. The projects are easy enough that both kids and adults can enjoy these recipes and crafts throughout the year. Above all, the projects in this book are sure to get an appreciative laugh or a nostalgic grin from everyone who's ever found a PEEPS Chick or Bunny in their Easter basket.

RECIPES

LITTLE PEEPS CUPCAKES

These buttery orange cupcakes topped with fluffy whipped cream and pink or blue Chicks make the perfect dessert for a baby shower. This recipe doubles easily to make 2 dozen cupcakes. You can decorate the cupcakes further with candy sprinkles, if you like. If crème fraîche is unavailable, use 1 ½ cups heavy cream.

FOR THE CUPCAKES:
$1/2$ cup unsalted butter, at room temperature
$3/4$ cup sugar
2 eggs
1 egg yolk
1 tablespoon vanilla extract
1 tablespoon grated orange zest
    (colored part of peel only)
$1 1/2$ cups all-purpose flour
$1 1/2$ teaspoons baking powder
$1/4$ teaspoon salt
$1/2$ cup milk

FOR THE FROSTING:
$3/4$ cup heavy cream
$3/4$ cup crème fraîche
2 tablespoons sugar
1 teaspoon vanilla extract

12 blue or pink PEEPS® Chicks

1. Preheat the oven to 350°F. Line a 12-cupcake tin with paper cupcake liners.

2. To make the cupcakes, with an electric mixer on medium-high speed, beat the butter and sugar in a bowl until light and fluffy, 4 to 5 minutes. Add the eggs and egg yolk, one at a

17

- - { recipe continues next page } - - -

time, beating well after each addition and scraping down the sides of the bowl as needed. Beat in the vanilla and the orange zest.

3. In another bowl, stir together the flour, baking powder, and salt.

4. Stir about one-third of the flour mixture into the butter mixture. Stir in half of the milk just until blended. Stir in half of the remaining flour mixture, then the remaining milk. Add the remaining flour mixture and stir just to blend.

5. Spoon the batter into the prepared cups.

6. Bake until a wooden skewer inserted into the center of a cupcake comes out clean, 15 to 18 minutes.

7. Transfer to a wire rack and let cool in the pan for 5 minutes, then remove the cupcakes from the pan and let cool completely on the rack before frosting.

8. To make the frosting, combine the cream, crème fraîche, sugar, and vanilla in a bowl. Using an electric mixer on high speed, beat until soft, fluffy peaks form.

9. When the cupcakes are completely cool, spread generously with the frosting. Top each with a Chick and serve immediately, or refrigerate in an airtight container for up to 8 hours.

MAKES 12 CUPCAKES

PEEPS MERINGUE TARTLETS

Toasted yellow Chicks take the place of meringue in these delightful lemon curd—filled mini tarts. You'll need twelve 3½- to 4-inch tartlet pans with removable bottoms to make this recipe. Watch carefully when you toast the Chicks; their yellow sugar coating will burn quickly! You can bake the tartlet shells up to two days ahead; store in an airtight container at room temperature.

½ cup unsalted butter, at room temperature
1 cup sugar
1 egg
2 cups all-purpose flour
¼ teaspoon salt
1 ½ cups (about 12 ounces) purchased lemon curd, or prepared lemon or vanilla pudding
12 yellow PEEPS® Chicks

1. In a large bowl, with an electric mixer on medium-high speed, beat the butter and sugar until well blended. Beat in the egg. In a small bowl, stir together the flour and salt. Stir the flour mixture into the butter mixture until well combined. Wrap the dough in wax paper or plastic wrap and refrigerate until firm, at least 2 hours and up to 1 week.

2. Divide the dough into 12 equal pieces. Press a dough piece over the bottom and up the sides to the rim of each of twelve 3 ½- to 4-inch tartlet pans with removable bottoms;

19

· · { recipe continues next page } · ·

the dough should be about $^1/_8$ inch thick. Place the dough-lined tartlet pans on a rimmed baking sheet. Cover with plastic wrap and freeze for 30 minutes. Meanwhile, preheat the oven to 350°F.

3. Transfer the baking sheet directly from the freezer to the oven (remove the plastic wrap) and bake the tartlet shells until golden brown, 16 to 18 minutes. Transfer to a wire rack and let cool on the baking sheet for about 10 minutes. Gently press the bottoms of the pans one at a time to release the tart shells and set them upright on the rack to cool completely.

4. Just before serving, preheat the oven to 400°F. Place the tartlet shells on a clean baking sheet and spoon about 2 tablespoons of the lemon curd into each. Place 1 Chick on each tartlet.

5. Bake for 1 to 2 minutes, just until the Chicks are slightly melted and starting to brown. Serve immediately.

MAKES 12 TARTLETS

One *PEEPS* Chick has 32 calories and 0 grams of fat. Please pass the *PEEPS*!

20

HALLOWEEN PARTY POUND CAKE

You swirl together chocolate and pumpkin batters to make a pretty Halloween-toned spiral in this moist pound cake, which combines with spooky PEEPS for a fun and tasty holiday table centerpiece.

FOR THE CAKE:

1 1/2 cups unsalted butter, at room temperature

3 cups sugar

6 eggs

2 teaspoons vanilla extract

1 1/4 cups canned pumpkin purée

2 3/4 cups all-purpose flour

2 teaspoons baking powder

1 teaspoon salt

1/2 teaspoon ground cinnamon

1/4 teaspoon ground nutmeg

1/8 teaspoon ground cloves

3/4 cup unsweetened Dutch-processed cocoa powder

2/3 cup buttermilk

FOR THE GLAZE:

4 ounces semisweet chocolate, chopped

1/2 cup heavy cream

1 tablespoon unsalted butter

1 teaspoon light corn syrup

12 PEEPS® Pumpkins

12 PEEPS® Ghosts

1. Preheat the oven to 350°F. Butter and flour a 12-cup Bundt or tube-cake pan.

2. In a large bowl, with an electric mixer on medium-high speed, beat the butter and sugar until light and fluffy, 4 to 5 minutes. Add the eggs, one at a time, beating well after each

·· { recipe continues next page } ··

addition and scraping down the sides of the bowl as needed. Beat in the vanilla. Scrape half of the butter mixture into another large bowl.

3. Make the pumpkin batter: Add the pumpkin purée to one of the bowls with half the butter mixture and stir until well blended. In a small bowl, stir together 1 $^3/_4$ cups of the flour, 1 teaspoon of the baking powder, $^1/_2$ teaspoon of the salt, and the cinnamon, nutmeg, and cloves. Stir the spiced flour mixture into the pumpkin mixture just until blended. Set aside.

4. Make the chocolate batter: In a small bowl, stir together the remaining 1 cup flour, 1 teaspoon baking powder, and $^1/_2$ teaspoon salt, and the cocoa powder. Stir about one-third of the cocoa-flour mixture into the bowl with the other half of the butter mixture. Stir in half of the buttermilk just until blended. Stir in half of the remaining flour mixture, then the remaining buttermilk. Add the remaining flour mixture and stir just to blend.

5. Spoon half of the pumpkin batter evenly into the bottom of the prepared pan. Spoon half of the chocolate batter over the pumpkin batter. Repeat to spoon the remaining pumpkin and chocolate batters into the pan. Gently run the blade of a butter knife around the pan several times to swirl the batters.

Just Born produces enough marshmallow candies in one year to circle the Earth twice.

6. Bake until a wooden skewer inserted into the center of the cake comes out with a few moist crumbs attached, 1 to 1 ^{1}/4 hours. Let cool in the pan for 10 minutes, then invert onto a serving platter and let cool completely.

7. While the cake cools, make the glaze: Place the chocolate, cream, butter, and corn syrup in a heatproof bowl set over a pan of barely simmering water. Stir frequently until the chocolate is melted and the glaze is smooth.

8. Spoon the warm glaze over the cake, letting it drip down the sides. Arrange the Pumpkins and Ghosts around the perimeter of the cake. Let stand until the glaze is set, about 2 hours. Cut into 12 large or 24 small wedges, each with one or two PEEPS.

MAKES 12 OR 24 SERVINGS

S'MORE PEEPS

Who says you need to be camping to make s'mores, and who says you have to use plain old marshmallows? Gooey, toasted PEEPS are the perfect choice for this campfire snack. Use the broiler or fireplace to toast the treats and camp out on the living room floor. Tent optional.

6 PEEPS® Chicks or Bunnies, any color

6 skewers or toasting forks

6 graham crackers, separated into 12 halves

Six 1-ounce squares semisweet chocolate

If you're gathered around a fire, place PEEPS on skewers and toast over the fire until warm and soft. Carefully transfer the melted PEEPS to graham cracker halves. Top each with a square of chocolate and a second graham cracker.

If you're using your oven, place a square of chocolate on a graham cracker square, top with a PEEPS candy, and place under the broiler for 30 to 60 seconds. Watch carefully to avoid burning, and when the PEEPS are melted to your satisfaction, top with a second cracker.

MAKES 6 S'MORES

PEEPS continues to be the #1 nonchocolate Easter candy in the United States—a distinction held for more than a decade.

PEEPS FONDUE

Invite a few friends over to channel the '70s fondue fad by dipping PEEPS in warm bittersweet chocolate. You don't even need a fancy fondue set—you can just use a saucepan and wooden BBQ skewers. If you like, for variety, add cubes of pound cake and some fruit, such as fresh strawberries and dried pear slices, to the platter.

1 1/2 cups heavy cream
1 pound bittersweet chocolate, finely chopped
24 PEEPS®, any shape or color

1. Bring the cream to a simmer in a saucepan. Reduce the heat to low.

2. Whisk in the chopped chocolate until the mixture is smooth. Remove the fondue from the heat.

3. Transfer the chocolate mixture to a fondue pot and place over the canned fuel burner or in a heatproof pot on a trivet over a votive candle, or serve the fondue straight from the saucepan. Arrange the PEEPS on a serving plate and offer fondue forks or wooden skewers to use for dipping.

MAKES 6 TO 8 SERVINGS

PEEPSICLES

There's nothing cuter than a PEEPS Pop. Many aficionados think that PEEPS taste best frozen—cold and creamy, and a bit chewy. These Bunnies are dipped in chocolate and rolled in coconut or chopped nuts, making them the ultimate frozen treat.

6 ounces semisweet chocolate, chopped
$^1/_2$ cup sweetened shredded coconut or $^1/_2$ cup peanuts (about 2 ounces), finely chopped
12 wooden craft sticks, available at candy-making–supply stores
12 PEEPS® Bunnies, any color

1. Line a baking sheet with wax paper.

2. Place the chocolate in a heatproof bowl set over a pan of barely simmering water. Stir occasionally until melted and smooth.

3. Place the coconut or nuts on a plate.

4. Insert 1 craft stick about halfway into the bottom section of 1 Bunny. Dip into the chocolate, turning to coat completely. Holding the dipped Bunny over the bowl of chocolate, use a knife to scrape the excess chocolate off the back and bottom of the Bunny, letting it fall back into the bowl. Hold the Bunny over the plate of coconut or nuts and sprinkle to cover all sides.

5. Place the Bunny on the prepared baking sheet and repeat to dip the remaining Bunnies. Freeze until firm, about 30 minutes. Serve frozen. PEEPSicles can be stored in an airtight container in the freezer for up to 1 week.

MAKES 12 PEEPSICLES

ORANGE HOT CHOCOLATE WITH PEEPS GHOSTS

Treat the ghouls and ghosts in your neighborhood on Halloween night with this rich orange-flavored cocoa. Orange oil is available at candy-making-supply stores and well-stocked grocery stores. If you can't find it, substitute orange extract. For a Christmas variation, substitute peppermint oil for the orange oil, and garnish with a PEEPS Tree.

1 ¼ cups whole or 2% milk
1 ounce bittersweet chocolate, finely chopped
1 to 2 drops orange oil or ¼ teaspoon orange extract
1 PEEPS® Ghost

1. In a small saucepan, heat the milk to a simmer. Remove from the heat and whisk in the chocolate until well blended. Whisk in the orange oil and pour into a large mug. Garnish with the Ghost and serve immediately.

MAKES 1 SERVING

PEEPS MAI TAI

A drink with a kitschy swizzle stick—is there anything better? One sip of this festive classic treat garnished with a parasol-twirling Bunny will transport you to the tropics. Hula your way to happiness with these virgin mai tais and PEEPS Leis (page 69) at the ultimate PEEPS-themed tiki party. To make a pitcher, just quadruple the recipe and stir together.

To mix an alcoholic option, replace the ginger ale with 1/4 cup light rum and 2 tablespoons dark rum.

1 wooden skewer, cut to a length of 5 inches

1 PEEPS® Bunny, any color

1 pineapple wedge

1 maraschino cherry

1 paper umbrella

Ice cubes

1 cup ginger ale

2 tablespoons fresh lime juice

1 tablespoon almond syrup

Splash of grenadine

1. Insert the skewer about halfway into the bottom section of the Bunny. Push the pineapple wedge and cherry onto the skewer until they are lined up just beneath the Bunny. Insert the paper umbrella into the side of the Bunny at a jaunty upright angle.

2. Fill a highball glass with ice. In a cocktail shaker, combine the ginger ale, lime juice, almond syrup, grenadine, and about 1 cup ice cubes. Shake well and strain into the prepared glass. Garnish with the Bunny skewer and serve.

MAKES 1 SERVING

PEEPS IN A BLANKET

Say "oui" to PEEPS tucked into cozy crêpe blankets and drizzled with orange-caramel sauce for a festive brunch. Serve some sliced strawberries on the side, if you like. Or, better yet, slice the straw-berries just so and give your Bunnies berets!

FOR THE ORANGE-CARAMEL SAUCE:
3/4 cup sugar
1/4 cup water
1 tablespoon corn syrup
1/4 cup heavy cream
1/4 cup orange juice

FOR THE CRÊPE BATTER:
3 large eggs
2/3 cup all-purpose flour
1 cup whole milk
2 tablespoons melted unsalted butter, plus more for the pan

1/2 cup orange marmalade
24 or 36 PEEPS® Bunnies, any color
Sliced strawberries for garnish (optional)

1. To make the orange-caramel sauce, in a small saucepan over medium-high heat, combine the sugar, water, and corn syrup and stir until the sugar has dissolved, 2 to 3 minutes. Raise the heat to high and boil, without stirring, until the syrup is a deep amber color, 3 to 5 minutes longer. Remove from the heat and carefully pour in the cream (be careful; the

37

{ recipe continues next page }

mixture will bubble up) and orange juice. Stir until smooth and well blended. Let the sauce cool before using, or cover and refrigerate for up to 2 weeks.

2. To make the crêpe batter, blend the eggs, flour, milk, and melted butter in a blender until smooth, scraping down the sides of the blender jar as needed.

3. Heat a 9-inch nonstick frying pan over medium heat; when hot, brush the bottom with butter, then wipe out any excess with a paper towel.

4. Lift the pan from the heat and pour in $1/4$ cup of the batter; tilt the pan and swirl the batter to coat the bottom. The crêpe should set at once and form tiny bubbles. Set the pan back over the heat and cook the crêpe until lightly browned at the edges, 1 to 3 minutes.

According to the 2007 PEEPS Celebrity Survey, people's favorite way to enjoy PEEPS is "head first," followed by "as decorations/crafts."

5. Run a spatula under the edge of the crêpe to loosen it. Turn the crêpe over and cook on the other side until lightly browned, about 1 minute longer, then slide onto a plate. Cover with a piece of wax paper. Repeat with the remaining batter, separating each crêpe with a piece of wax paper; you should have 12 crêpes.

6. To serve, spread a crêpe with about 2 teaspoons of the marmalade. Arrange 2 or 3 Bunnies along the center of the crêpe. Roll up the crêpe around the Bunnies. Place 2 filled crêpes on each of 6 individual plates. Drizzle with the orange-caramel sauce and serve.

MAKES 12 CREPES; SERVES 6

MOLTEN CHOCOLATE PEEPS CAKES

Everybody loves warm, bittersweet, molten chocolate cake. Why not melt a PEEPS Chick into the center? These rich, puddinglike cakes are slightly underbaked and served in their ramekins, as the melted marshmallow makes them too gooey to stand alone. If you don't have ramekins, bake and serve each cake in a small ovenproof bowl instead.

8 ounces bittersweet chocolate, finely chopped
4 tablespoons unsalted butter
6 tablespoons sugar
4 egg yolks
1/4 cup all-purpose flour
2 egg whites
6 PEEPS® Chicks

1. Preheat the oven to 350°F.

2. Place the chocolate and butter in a heatproof bowl set over a pan of simmering water. Stir frequently until the mixture is melted and smooth. Remove the bowl from the heat and whisk in 4 tablespoons of the sugar and the egg yolks. Whisk in the flour.

{ recipe continues next page }

3. In a bowl, with an electric mixer on high speed, beat the egg whites until frothy. With the mixer running, add the remaining 2 tablespoons sugar in a slow, steady stream. Continue beating just until soft peaks form. Fold about one-third of the egg whites into the chocolate mixture to lighten it, then gently fold in the remaining whites until no streaks remain.

4. Divide the mixture evenly among six 4-ounce ramekins or ovenproof bowls. Place a Chick in the center of each ramekin, pressing to submerge (it's okay if the Chicks show a bit through the surface of the batter).

5. Bake just until the tops of the cakes are puffed up and dry to the touch, 12 to 15 minutes. Let cool for about 10 minutes, then serve warm.

MAKES 6 SERVINGS

Just Born's founder, Sam Born, is also known for having invented chocolate sprinkles and a machine that inserts sticks into lollipops.

PEEPS AFTER DARK

PEEPS aren't just for the kids' Easter baskets! Dress up a few with a coating of dark chocolate and a sprinkle of edible gold powder for a fancy dinner party. Wooden skewers, paper candy cups, and gold dusting powder are available at candy-making supply stores.

Note: The FDA classifies gold dusting powder as a nontoxic product for decorative use only. However, candy makers use it to gild their confections. If you'd rather not use it on your PEEPS, try sprinkling them with clear sparkling sugar instead. You'll lose a little luster, but none of the sophistication.

6 ounces bittersweet or semisweet chocolate, chopped
1 or 2 wooden skewers
12 PEEPS® Bunnies or Chicks, any color
Edible gold dusting powder (optional; see Note)

1. Line a baking sheet with wax paper. Place the chocolate in a heatproof bowl set over a pan of barely simmering water. Stir frequently until the chocolate is melted and smooth.

2. Insert a wooden skewer about halfway into the bottom section of 1 Bunny. Dip into the chocolate, turning to coat completely. Holding the dipped Bunny over the bowl of chocolate, use a knife to scrape the excess chocolate off the back and bottom of the Bunny, letting it fall back into bowl. Place the Bunny on the prepared baking sheet and gently remove the skewer.

43

· · { recipe continues next page } · ·

3. Repeat to dip the remaining Bunnies. Refrigerate until the chocolate is set, about 1 hour.

4. Place each Bunny in a fluted candy cup and dust lightly with the gold dust, if using. Store in an airtight container in the refrigerator for up to 1 week.

MAKES 12 CHOCOLATE-COVERED PEEPS

> Guinness no longer sanctions records of food consumption. But, according to Internet lore, the world record for PEEPS consumption is 72 in 30 minutes.

PEEPS IN NESTS

Peep peep! In this recipe, Chicks keep jelly-bean eggs cozy in coconut macaroon nests. Serve these cute cookies for dessert, or use them as table favors for a spring feast. Speckled jelly beans give you the most realistic look, but any color will do the trick.

2 eggs
1/2 cup sugar
1 teaspoon vanilla
3 1/2 cups sweetened flaked coconut
1/4 cup all-purpose flour
36 TEENEE BEANEE® jelly beans
12 yellow or pink PEEPS® Chicks

1. Preheat the oven to 350°F. Butter a baking sheet or line with parchment baking paper.

2. In a bowl, with an electric mixer on high speed, beat the eggs, sugar, and vanilla until pale and frothy, 3 to 4 minutes. Stir in the coconut and flour until well blended.

3. To make the nests, make 12 mounds of about 3 tablespoons batter each, placing them about 2 inches apart on the baking sheet. Use a spoon to spread each mound into a 2 1/2-inch circle with a depression in the center.

4. Bake until the nests are golden brown, about 20 minutes. Remove from the oven and carefully press 3 jelly beans into the center of each nest. Use a spatula to transfer the nests to a wire rack to cool completely. Store the nests in an airtight container at room temperature for up to 2 days. Top each nest with a Chick just before serving.

MAKES 12 COOKIES

PEEPS AFFOGATO

Can't do without your shot of caffeine in the morning? Pining for a sugar boost in the late afternoon? Combine the two with a PEEPS Chick splashed with a shot of hot espresso, and give a whole new meaning to "caffeine buzz." Don't forget a little coffee spoon for scooping up any remaining sugary dregs in the bottom of the cup.

1 shot hot espresso
1 PEEPS® Chick, any color

1. Place the Chick snugly in an espresso or demitasse cup. Pour the espresso over the Chick and drink immediately.

MAKES 1 SERVING

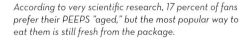

According to very scientific research, 17 percent of fans prefer their PEEPS "aged," but the most popular way to eat them is still fresh from the package.

CRAFTS

PEEPS CHOPSTICK RESTS

A PEEPS Chick, wrapped nigiri-sushi style with a thin band of origami paper, will make a great resting place for everyone's chopsticks at your next sushi dinner. If you plan to eat the PEEPS after dinner (recommended!), use tape to secure the origami paper rather than glue.

YOU WILL NEED:
Origami paper in assorted patterns
Ruler
Scissors
Glue stick or double-sided tape
6 yellow PEEPS® Chicks

1. Cut 6 strips of origami paper approximately 4 1/2 inches long and 1/4 inch wide. Apply glue or a trimmed piece of double-sided tape to the underside of one end of a strip. Wrap the strip around the chest of 1 Chick, just under the beak. Overlap the ends and press gently to adhere. Repeat with the remaining Chicks.

2. Place a Chick next to each place setting and prop chopsticks across the Chicks' tails.

MAKES 6 CHOPSTICK RESTS

PEEPS CHECKERS

You'll want to bring out this game board every Easter. The rules are the same as they are in regular checkers, except that you get to eat any game pieces you capture. Gold paper fluted candy cups cut as shown and placed on the Chicks' heads are a nice way to "king" the playing pieces.

Note: Foam core board is available in a variety of colors at large art-supply stores. Possible color schemes for the checkerboard are pink and yellow, blue and yellow, or blue and pink. Just be sure to choose a paint color that is darker than the color of the foam core board, and then buy 12 PEEPS in each color to use as the playing pieces.

This craft involves using sharp instruments for cutting. Please make sure children have adult supervision if they are going to make this project.

YOU WILL NEED:

X-Acto knife

20-inch square pink, light blue, or yellow foam core board

Ruler

Pencil

1 piece thin cardboard, preferably chipboard (about 8 $1/2$ by 11 inches)

Blue or pink acrylic paint

Angle-tipped paintbrush, about $1/4$ inch wide

12 PEEPS® Chicks in each of 2 colors (24 total)

Gold paper fluted candy cups (optional)

1. Use the X-Acto knife to trim the foam core board into a 20-inch square, if necessary.

2. Use the ruler and pencil to mark the board into sixty-four 2 $1/2$-inch squares, 8 across and 8 up and down.

54

· · · { craft continues next page } · · ·

3. Using the cardboard as a guide, carefully paint every other square so that you have a checkerboard pattern. Let dry for about 30 minutes, then touch up with a second coat if necessary.

4. Let dry completely. Assemble your PEEPS on the board and let the games begin. Place gold paper fluted candy cups on a Chick's head when "kinging" it, if desired.

MAKES 1 PEEPS CHECKERBOARD WITH PLAYERS

In the early 1950s, it took 27 hours to make a single PEEPS Chick. With today's special machines, it takes 6 minutes. Three cheers for assembly lines!

PEEPS WEDDING CAKE TOPPER

They're already joined at the hip—dress them up with a little bow tie and a wedding veil, and you've got the sweetest couple ever to grace the top of a wedding cake! These cake toppers would be adorable on cupcakes at a wedding shower, too. Ask for a sample of wedding veil tulle fabric at a fabric or craft store; many stores are happy to snip you off a little piece at no charge.

YOU WILL NEED:

Scissors

1 or 2 sprigs small silk flowers on wire stems

One 4-by-2-inch piece white tulle fabric

2 PEEPS® Chicks, any color

Black construction paper

Hot-glue gun and glue sticks

Note: This craft involves using a hot-glue gun. Please make sure children have adult supervision if they are going to make this project.

57

· · · { craft continues next page } · · ·

1. Snip apart the flower sprig(s), leaving about 1/4 inch of wire stem attached to each flower.

2. Fold the long end of the tulle fabric scrap accordion style and attach to 1 Chick's head, using flowers as pins. Press a few additional flowers into the Chick's chest, for a bouquet.

3. Cut a bow tie out of the black construction paper and attach to the other Chick's neck with the hot glue.

4. Press lightly into icing to affix to cake or cupcakes.

MAKES 1 WEDDING CAKE TOPPER

There are more than 200 unofficial PEEPS fan Web sites. That's a lot of PEEPS fans in cyberspace!

PEEPS PLACE-CARD HOLDERS

Place-card holders let everyone know where to sit at a formal table setting, but nothing says they have to be stuffy. Add a little whimsy to the table with colorful PEEPS Chicks (mix colors for a festive look, or choose one color to complement your table setting). Best of all, guests can eat them after the meal.

YOU WILL NEED:
Scissors
White or cream-colored card stock or heavy paper
Black, brown, or metallic silver or gold pen
Decorations, such as PEEPS® foam craft stickers from Darice (optional)
Paring knife or serrated utility knife
8 PEEPS® Chicks, any color

1. Cut eight 2-by-3 $1/2$-inch rectangles out of the card stock and write each guest's name on a card. Decorate as you like.

2. With a sharp knife, make a slice on the back of each Chick's head just behind the eyes, across the entire width and about $1/2$ inch deep.

60

· · { craft continues next page } · ·

3. Pinch the sides of each Chick's head to open the gap and insert a place card. The sticky marshmallow will hold the card securely.

4. Place a Chick place-card holder in the center of each plate, or at the head of each place setting, if you prefer.

MAKES 8 PLACE-CARD HOLDERS

According to the 2007 PEEPS Celebrity Survey, 59 percent of people think the Chick is cooler than the Bunny.

GARLAND of PEEPS

A swag of colorful candy and satin bows makes an eye-catching mantle or table decoration for any holiday. Substitute Ghosts at Halloween, or Snowmen and Trees at Christmas. You can adjust these instructions to make a garland the length of your choice. If you plan to use it on a table, allow for extra length to curve around platters, candles, or centerpieces.

YOU WILL NEED:

5 feet of ³/₄- to 1-inch-wide satin ribbon

Scissors

Nylon-coated bead-stringing wire
  or waxed twine

Large embroidery or tapestry needle

Paper towels

Vegetable oil

Hot-glue gun and glue sticks

About 1 pound TEENEE BEANEE® jelly beans

10 to 20 PEEPS® Chicks or Bunnies, any color

Note: This craft involves using a hot-glue gun. Please make sure children have adult supervision if they are going to make this project.

1. Cut the ribbon into 3 equal lengths and tie each piece into a bow.

2. Measure out about 5 feet of wire. Tie a knot about 2 inches from one end of the length of wire. Thread the other end through the tapestry needle. Use a paper towel to lightly coat the wire and needle with oil (reapply oil as needed when the needle or wire becomes sticky).

63

{ craft continues next page }

3. String 1 bow on the wire, pushing it to the end flush with the knot, then apply a dab of hot glue to the knot and affix it to the back of the bow to hold it in place. String on some of the jelly beans and PEEPS, alternating shapes and colors as desired. At the midway point, tie a knot and string another bow. Hot-glue the knot to the second bow. String the rest of the garland to about 2 inches from the end of the wire. String the last bow and knot the end securely. Hot-glue the knot to the final bow.

MAKES ONE 4-FOOT-LONG GARLAND

According to the 2007 PEEPS Celebrity Survey, Will Ferrell is the male celebrity who most closely resembles PEEPS candy (either in physique, colorful attire, or sweet nature/personality).

PEEPS SPRING TABLE CENTERPIECE

Arrange an Easter table centerpiece that really makes a statement by surrounding a small vase of flowers with a larger vase filled with Bunnies or Chicks. Combine several colors for a festive spring look, or stick to one or two colors if you're going for understated elegance.

YOU WILL NEED:

1 large glass vase, preferably with a large mouth and a clean, modern shape

1 thinner vase that fits inside the large vase with at least 1 inch of room on all sides

Cut big-blossomed flowers such as Easter lilies, peonies, or hyacinths

10 to 20 PEEPS® Bunnies or Chicks per quart of vase volume, any color

1. Fill the smaller vase with a few inches of water. Carefully place the small vase inside the large vase and arrange the cut flowers in the smaller vase.

2. Fill the space between the small vase and the large vase with PEEPS, arranging them so that they face outward and hide the smaller vase.

MAKES 1 CENTERPIECE

PEEPS LEIS

Host a PEEPS-themed luau and set out materials for guests to make their own colorful leis. Inexpensive fabric flower leis are available at party stores. Don't forget to serve up a tray of PEEPS Mai Tais (page 34).

YOU WILL NEED:
6 fabric flower leis, in various colors
Scissors
Nylon-coated bead-stringing wire
Measuring tape
Large embroidery or tapestry needle
Paper towels
Vegetable oil
About 100 PEEPS® Bunnies or Chicks, any color

1. Take the flower leis apart by snipping the string, and remove the flowers. Measure out six 40-inch pieces of the bead stringing wire.

2. Tie a knot about 2 inches from one end of a piece of wire. Thread the other end through the tapestry needle. Use a paper towel to lightly coat the wire and needle with oil (reapply oil as needed when the needle or wire become sticky).

3. String on the flowers and PEEPS, alternating a Chick or Bunny for every 6 to 8 flowers, until you have about 2 inches of wire remaining. Knot the ends securely. Repeat to make the remaining leis.

SUGAR COOKIE PEEPS COOP

PEEPS Chicks roost on tinted coconut hay in this barnyard version of a gingerbread house. You can bake the sugar cookie pieces a day or two ahead (store in airtight containers at room temperature). Any kind of food coloring will work, but gel food colors are much more vivid than their liquid counterparts; find them in stores that carry baking and cake-decorating supplies. You'll use 1 batch of icing to assemble the coop and another batch to decorate it.

YOU WILL NEED:

1 batch Sugar Cookie Dough (page 76)
PEEPS® Coop Templates (pages 94–95)
Sharp knife
2 batches Royal Icing (page 77)
3 pastry bags fitted with a ¹/₄-inch plain tip
  or 3 zip-top plastic bags with 1 corner snipped
  to make a ¹/₄-inch hole

9-by-12-inch cardboard rectangle
Red, black, and yellow food coloring
1 cup sweetened flaked coconut
Several PEEPS® Chicks, any color, and
  assorted colorful candies of your choice

1. Preheat the oven to 350°F. Butter 2 baking sheets or line with parchment baking paper.

2. On a lightly floured board, with a lightly floured rolling pin, roll out one-third of the dough ¹/₄ to ¹/₈ inch thick.

70

· · · { craft continues next page } · · ·

3. Place pattern A on top of the dough and, using the tip of a sharp knife, cut around the pattern to make the front wall of the coop. Carefully transfer to a prepared baking sheet.

4. Repeat to make a second pattern A, for the back wall; 2 pattern B's for the side-wall pieces; and 2 pattern C's for the roof pieces. Use the template to cut 3 doorways, each about 1 1/2 by 2 inches, evenly spaced, in one of the side-wall pieces, and place the cut-out doors on the baking sheet as well.

5. Bake until golden brown around the edges, 10 to 13 minutes, rotating the position of the pans midway through the baking time. Let the pieces cool completely on the pans. Meanwhile, make the Royal Icing.

6. To assemble the coop, fill a pastry or zip-top bag with icing. Pipe a generous strip of icing along the bottom edge of the front-wall piece (pattern A) of the coop. Stand the wall up with the iced edge on the cardboard base where you want the front of the coop, and prop up with jars or cans until the icing has hardened, about 5 minutes.

7. To attach the first side wall (B), pipe icing along bottom edge and along the inside of one side edge. Attach the side wall carefully to the front wall (side wall pieces will fit over the outside edges of the front and back pieces), pressing gently to adhere. Let dry about 5 minutes.

The machines at the Just Born factory can add 3,800 PEEPS eyes per minute! Here's looking at you, Chick.

8. Use the same technique to attach the second side wall (B) and the back wall (A). Pipe additional icing along the inside seams of the coop and let dry for at least 10 minutes before attaching the roof.

9. To attach the roof, pipe a strip of icing along the top edges of all 4 walls of the coop. Gently press each roof piece (C) into the icing so that the top edges butt to form a peak and the bottom edges overhang the side walls slightly. Pipe additional icing along the top seam of the roof. Use tall cans or jars to prop up the roof as it dries, if necessary. Let the coop dry completely, several hours or overnight, before decorating the outside.

10. To decorate the coop, spoon about half a batch of icing into a bowl and color with red food coloring. Divide the remaining icing in half again, place each portion in a small bowl, and color one portion light gray with a few drops of black food coloring. Leave the remaining icing white.

11. Spoon the red icing into a clean pastry or zip-top bag. Carefully pipe the red icing onto the coop to decorate the walls. It's easiest if you pipe an outline and some generous dollops of icing first, and then use a small butter knife or offset spatula to spread the icing evenly. Decorate the coop doors separately, icing them on 1 side with red. Press each gently into the front wall over a doorway, icing side up (see photo on page 74).

73

· · · { *craft continues next page* } · ·

12. Spoon the gray icing into another clean bag and use the same technique to decorate the roof. Put the white icing in the original (also white) bag (or a new bag if you assembled the coop ahead of time) and pipe a white windowpane pattern on the doors; use the white icing to draw doors on the side walls as well, if you like. Spread the remaining white icing on the floor of the coop in the doorways and on the surrounding cardboard (see photo on the facing page).

13. Put the coconut in a small bowl. Add a few drops of yellow food coloring and mix until the color is uniformly distributed. Sprinkle the white icing on the floor and "ground" with coconut.

14. Add PEEPS and other candy as desired.

MAKES 1 SUGAR COOKIE COOP

In 2007, green was added to the Easter assortment, replacing white.

PEEPS Chicks and Bunnies come in five colors.

The classic yellow Chicks are the most popular, followed by pink, lavender, blue, and green.

75

SUGAR COOKIE DOUGH

*This recipe makes enough dough for one PEEPS Coop,
with enough to bake a few extra pieces in case of breakage.*

1 cup unsalted butter, at room temperature

2 cups sugar

2 eggs

4 cups all-purpose flour

$\frac{1}{2}$ teaspoon baking powder

$\frac{1}{2}$ teaspoon salt

1. In a bowl, with an electric mixer on medium speed, beat the butter and sugar until well blended. Beat in the eggs.

2. In a small bowl, stir together the flour, baking powder, and salt.

3. Stir the flour mixture into the butter mixture until well combined. Use immediately, or wrap tightly in plastic wrap and refrigerate for up to 1 week.

MAKES 1 PEEPS COOP OR ABOUT FORTY-EIGHT 4-INCH COOKIES

ROYAL ICING

This edible icing dries very hard, making it perfect for assembling and decorating cookie buildings. You can mix the icing up to 30 minutes ahead of time. Cover any that you're not using with plastic wrap so that it doesn't dry out. Instead of salmonella-risky raw egg whites, this recipe uses meringue powder, available in stores that carry baking and cake-decorating supplies.

3 cups powdered sugar
1/4 cup meringue powder
3 to 4 tablespoons warm water

1. Mix the powdered sugar, meringue powder, and water until the icing is a thick, spreadable consistency. If the mixture is too thick, add a few more drops of water; if too thin, stir in more powdered sugar.

MAKES 4 CUPS

PEEPS HOLIDAY WREATH

Deck the halls with boughs of PEEPS! In this wreath, marshmallow Trees or Snowmen replace evergreen branches. If you like, add red candies for the berries and you have a festive winter wreath.

YOU WILL NEED:

One 8-inch Styrofoam wreath form

1 can spray paint (optional)

Hot-glue gun and glue sticks

About 35 PEEPS® Trees or Snowmen

About 2 dozen red MIKE AND IKE®
  or HOT TAMALES® candies (optional)

Thin wire for hanging

About 2 feet of 1-inch-wide satin ribbon

1. Lay the wreath form flat on a work surface. If your wreath form is white, or some other color you don't want to show through little cracks between the PEEPS, spray paint it a solid color of your choice. Be sure to do so outside or in a well-ventilated area. Then, beginning on the inside edge of the wreath form, apply a generous amount of hot glue to the back of a Tree and glue it securely lengthwise to the Styrofoam (see photo); repeat as needed.

2. Working toward the outside edge of the wreath form, glue 2 or 3 Trees perpendicular to each Tree around the inside edge, to make a crosswise band of Trees around that section of the wreath, fitting the Trees as snugly together as possible. Continue to make bands of Trees in the same way all around the wreath, butting each new row snugly against the previous one (see photo). When finished, hot-glue red chewy candies into any visible space, if desired.

3. Attach a loop of wire for hanging at the top. Tie the ribbon into a bow and attach with hot glue at the bottom of the wreath. Hang the wreath indoors; PEEPS don't like the cold and damp!

MAKES 1 HOLIDAY WREATH

PEEPS PRINTED CANVAS TOTE

Use PEEPS and fabric paints to turn blank canvas totes into Easter basket-bags printed with pink, yellow, and blue Bunnies. Or make trick-or-treat bags printed with glow-in-the-dark Ghosts. Cheaptotes.com is a great resource for natural or colored cotton totes. If you want to expand your choices of paint colors, you can make acrylic paint suitable for printing on fabrics by mixing it with fabric paint medium, about 1 part fabric medium to 2 parts paint.

YOU WILL NEED:
Pencil and paper
PEEPS®, any color or shape
Cotton tote bag, prewashed and ironed
1 piece cardboard, small enough to fit inside the tote but large enough to cover your entire design
Fabric paint, any and as many colors as you like
Shallow dish(es) or bowl(s)
Small paintbrush

1. Using the pencil and paper, make a sketch ahead of time to plan your print design.

2. Separate the PEEPS carefully to preserve their shape and choose the ones with the most distinct outlines to use for making prints.

· · · { craft continues next page } · · ·

3. Place the tote bag on a flat surface and insert the cardboard inside to keep the paint from soaking through.

4. Pour the fabric paint into a shallow dish, or dishes if using multiple colors.

5. Dip the front side of one of your PEEPS in paint to coat. Make a few test prints ahead of time, so you can get a feel for how thickly you should coat the PEEPS with the paint. To print on the fabric, place PEEPS, paint side down, onto the tote and press gently. Lift off carefully. Touch up the print with the paintbrush, if necessary, and add eyes and noses using black paint.

6. Repeat the process as desired. The PEEPS should each make several prints.

7. Let the tote dry for 24 hours before using.

MAKES 1 TOTE

PEEPIÑATA

This egg-shaped piñata (filled with PEEPS, of course) is a terrific party starter for your favorite PEEPS lover's next bash. Plus, it's super messy, so kids will love to get involved. Note that it takes a few days to dry, so plan ahead. And make quick work of the cleanup by using disposable square aluminum baking pans for mixing the papier-mâché paste.

Note: This craft involves using a hot-glue gun. Please make sure children have adult supervision if they are going to make this project.

YOU WILL NEED:

Several days' worth of old newspapers
One 17-inch round balloon
4 cups flour
2 teaspoons salt
4 to 4 1/2 cups warm water
Disposable plastic or aluminum container
Masking tape
About ten 5-count packages assorted PEEPS® (for filling)

Paintbrush
Colorful tempera (poster) paint (pink, yellow, blue, purple, etc.)
20 to 30 PEEPS® Chicks or Bunnies, any color (for decoration)
Ribbon and other decorations (optional)
Hot-glue gun and glue sticks
Thin wire and string for hanging

1. Spread a large work surface with newspapers or a plastic drop cloth. Tear newspapers into 1-inch-wide strips. Strips that are between 6 and 12 inches long are easiest to work with.

2. Blow up and tie off the balloon.

3. To make 1 batch of papier-mâché paste, stir together 2 cups flour, 1 teaspoon salt, and 2 to 2 1/4 cups warm water until you have a smooth paste about the consistency of yogurt.

- - { craft continues next page } - -

4. Draw a strip of newspaper through the paste, wiping off the excess with your fingers. Place the strip across the balloon at an angle. Repeat, laying strips on the same angle and slightly overlapping, until the entire balloon is covered except for an opening with a diameter of about 4 inches around the knot of the balloon. Set aside to dry.

5. Once dry, repeat with a second layer of newspaper strips dredged in paste, angling the strips perpendicular to the first layer. (Angling the strips provides structural support and also makes it easier to distinguish between layers as you go.) Once the balloon is coated with a second layer of strips, repeat with a third layer, and then a fourth. (After the first layer of strips, it does not need to dry between each additional layer.) Let dry completely, 1 to 2 days.

6. Puncture and remove the balloon. Fill the balloon with wrapped packages of PEEPS, and then use masking tape to cover the opening.

7. Mix a second batch of papier-mâché paste and apply more newspaper strips dredged in paste to secure the opening. Let dry completely.

8. Paint the egg with desired color. When the paint is dry, attach PEEPS, notions, glitter, or any decorations you like with the hot glue.

9. To hang, make two small holes on top of the egg and run wire though the holes to make a loop. Run a long string through the loop to hang.

RESOURCES

Peeps BRAND marshmallow candies are available at most retail locations, especially around the holidays. But seasonal shapes can be tricky to find out-of-season, so stock up when you can and take advantage of these craft and recipe ideas all year long. If you absolutely *must* have a PEEPS Ghost garland in July, you can always try your luck on eBay. Even if you don't find the shape you're looking for, you'll have fun browsing more PEEPS paraphernalia than you could ever imagine.

The facing page lists some online resources for the other ingredients and materials you'll need to make the recipes and crafts in this book.

AMERICAN SPOON

www.spoon.com

Marmalade and other high-quality preserves.

THE BAKER'S CATALOGUE

www.bakerscatalogue.com

High-quality flours including unbleached all-purpose, cake, and pastry flours; lemon curd; chocolate; and baking equipment.

BLICK ART MATERIALS

www.dickblick.com

Paints, paintbrushes, fabric paint medium.

CANDYLAND CRAFTS

www.candylandcrafts.com

Candy-making, cake-decorating, and baking supplies including pans and molds, food coloring, edible glitter, and meringue powder; and Wilton decorating supplies.

CHEAP JOE'S ART STUFF

www.cheapjoes.com

Paints, paintbrushes, fabric paint medium.

CHEAPTOTES

www.cheaptotes.com

Canvas tote bags in a variety of colors and sizes.

COOK FLAVORING COMPANY

www.cooksvanilla.com

Top-quality vanilla and other extracts, such as peppermint and orange.

JO-ANN FABRICS

www.joann.com

Craft supplies including cake-making materials, wreath forms, fabric, ribbons, and tons of other notions.

MICHAELS

www.michaels.com

Craft supplies including craft sticks, wreath forms, fabric, and ribbons; candy-making supplies including paper candy cups; food-color sprays and markers; and an extensive line of Wilton products.

SWEET CELEBRATIONS

www.sweetc.com

(Formerly Maid of Scandinavia.) Huge assortment of cookie cutters, presses, and molds; decorating sugars; flavorings; and chocolate.

WILLIAMS-SONOMA

www.williams-sonoma.com

Tartlet pans, Bundt and tube pans, ramekins, and other baking equipment.

WILTON INDUSTRIES

www.wilton.com

Extensive selection of bakeware and decorating supplies.

INDEX